partnerships for learning

a guide to evaluating arts education projects

by Felicity Woolf

Contents

Introduction

The aims of the guide

Partnerships for learning aims to help everyone involved in arts education projects to understand evaluation clearly and to evaluate effectively, according to their particular needs. In the long term, the aim of the guide is to raise the standard of arts education projects.

Arts-based projects are difficult to evaluate and the guide does not try to suggest that there is only one way of approaching evaluation. It aims to provide a flexible framework, which can be applied in many different situations and used to evaluate short or more extended projects. *Partnerships for learning* is for everyone; whether you are experienced in evaluation techniques or an absolute beginner the guide is designed to help you get the most out of the time you invest in evaluating your project.

Evaluating the quality of the creative process is open to argument and interpretation and the guide suggests a range of measures of success for creative projects, with the emphasis on flexibility and fitness for purpose.

Using the guide

The guide can be read in its entirety, or you can dip into it, to get advice on particular aspects of evaluation. The guide is designed to be used in different ways.

You do not need to evaluate every aspect of your project in-depth, but can use the guide to help you focus on one or two areas, according to your needs. Many pages are photocopiable, and wherever possible key concepts, ideas and questions are highlighted so that they can be easily picked out and used at meetings or in training sessions.

You may find it helpful to look at Appendix 1, which is a quick reference guide to evaluation practice. This may help you decide which sections of the guide will be most useful to you.

The development of the guide

The guide was developed by Felicity Woolf after extensive consultation with artists, arts organisations, youth and community group leaders, teachers, arts advisers and local authority officers. It was piloted in draft form by 18 groups and organisations throughout England, and many of the examples included came from these pilot projects. A list of the pilot groups is included in Appendix 4. Felicity Woolf also devised and delivered a national programme of training with support materials, which ran alongside the distribution of the first edition of the guide. Feedback from these training sessions and other evidence gathered over the last five years have contributed to this second edition.

Equal opportunities

Evaluation should give everyone involved in an arts project the opportunity to contribute their views about it. No one should be excluded from this process because of their race, gender, sexual orientation, social background or disability.

Arts Council England strongly advocates creative approaches to evaluation which can allow potentially excluded groups, including those with limited communication skills, to contribute their views.

Who is the guide for?

The guide will be useful to anyone who organises, funds, delivers or takes part in arts projects which aim to have learning outcomes. In the guide, these groups or individuals are called partners, in the belief that the principle of partnership forms the basis of all arts projects.

Partners might be:

- adult learners
- artists and arts organisations
- arts funders
- children and young people
- community workers

- early years practitioners
- local authority officers
- teachers
- voluntary groups
- youth leaders

What kinds of arts projects?

The guide is to help partners evaluate arts-led projects in the context of lifelong learning, which aim to do one or more of the following:

- increase knowledge and understanding of the arts
- develop arts skills
- develop creativity
- bring about personal and social change through the arts and creativity

Arts-led education projects can be part of a formal curriculum or part of informal activity. They can take place in many different contexts, for example at a school, pupil referral unit, youth club, young offenders' institution, community or voluntary group, or they may be part of the education and access programme of an arts organisation.

In the guide the term 'arts' is used for any arts activity.
It includes all kinds of:

- combined arts
- film and video
- media, writing and broadcast arts
- multimedia and digital technology
- performing arts
- visual arts and crafts

An artist can be working in any, or a combination of, these art forms.

What is evaluation?

Evaluation is a powerful tool for learning. It is a structured way of thinking about what happens during your project, and why. It can be simple or complex, depending on the resources you have available, and on what you want to find out. We suggest that evaluation is based on the following three key ideas.

- Evaluation involves making judgements, based on evidence, about the value and quality of a project.
- Evaluation is open and clear and involves all partners, including the people taking part.
- Evaluation helps with decision-making during a project and for future projects.

This guide focuses on helping partners to evaluate their own projects, but there may be reasons for appointing an external evaluator, such as lack of time. An external evaluator may be seen as more objective, which may be important for some partnerships. Appendix 2 shows the advantages and disadvantages of appointing an external evaluator.

Why evaluate?

Evaluation has two main purposes:

- to improve practice during the project and for future projects

- to show what happened as a result of a project

Improving is important so that:

- projects can evolve and change as they happen
- partners like artists, group leaders and participants feel the evaluation is for their benefit, and not just for funders
- projects can be better next time and standards raised
- partners can change and develop their practice

It is important to show:

- that arts projects are a good way of learning
- how everyone benefited from the project
- that funding has been well used

How the guide is organised

Five stages of evaluation

The guide divides evaluation into five stages.

1. Planning
2. Collecting evidence
3. Assembling and interpreting
4. Reflecting and moving forward
5. Reporting and sharing

However, evaluation is rarely a linear process. The results of analysing evidence at Stage 3 and of reflecting at Stage 4, may well lead to going back to Stages 1 and 2, and making changes to objectives or to the way evidence is collected.

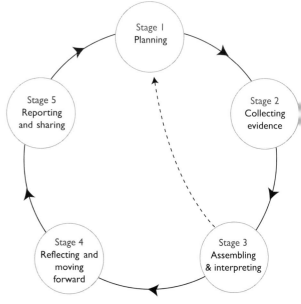

Stage 1 Planning

Stage 2 Collecting evidence

Stage 3 Assembling & interpreting

Stage 4 Reflecting and moving forward

Stage 5 Reporting and sharing

Focus questions

Stage 1 - Planning
Why are we doing this project?
What specific things do we want to achieve?
How will we identify success?

Stage 2 - Collecting evidence
How will we collect the evidence we need?

Stage 3 - Assembling and interpreting
What does the evidence tell us?

Stage 4 - Reflecting and moving forward
What have we learned from the evaluation?
How will we do things differently in future?

Stage 5 - Reporting and sharing
Who will we tell about the project and why?
How will we tell them?
What will we tell them?

Contents of the guide

Each section includes:

- focus questions
- a discussion of key issues
- examples illustrating key concepts and tables summarising information
- a summary checklist

All five summary checklists are brought together for quick reference on page 48.

A glossary on starting on page 67 explains some of the specialist terms used in the guide, although these are also explained in the text when they are first used.

There are six appendices.

- Appendix 1, Setting standards for evaluation: self-review, will help you review how well you evaluate projects, and should bring out areas which you need to strengthen. It is best consulted before you evaluate a new project.

- Appendix 2, External and internal evaluation: advantages and disadvantages, helps you consider whether to appoint someone from outside the partnership to lead on evaluating your project.

- Appendix 3, Techniques for collecting evidence, gives more information about the different ways of collecting evidence, which are introduced in Stage 2.

- Appendix 4, Pilot groups, lists the groups and organisations which piloted the guide.

- Appendix 5, Contacting the Arts Council England.

- Appendix 6, Additional resources, suggests further reading and useful websites.

Stage 1 Planning

Planning to evaluate

Good planning is vital for effective evaluation, whatever the scale of your project. You need to think about evaluation from the very beginning, along with other practical details. Evaluation needs to be programmed into your schedule, so that time is allowed for all the stages of the process. If you don't think about evaluation until the end of your project, you may miss important evidence or find it more difficult to collect.

You also need to include evaluation in the project budget, as it takes time and resources. For example, freelance artists should be paid for attending evaluation meetings

At the planning stage, think about:

- Who will have overall responsibility for evaluation?
- Who else will have a role in collecting evidence?
- How much will evaluation cost in time and money?
- Has evaluation been included in the budget?
- How will you collect the evidence you need? (This is dealt with in detail in Stage 2, but needs to be considered as part of the planning process.)
- When will you review the project? (This is dealt with in detail in Stage 3, but review sessions during and after the project need to be included in the project timetable.)

For example, **Puffins Nursery** organised a 10-week music and dance education project which included all evaluation costs in the budget outline. The total cost of the project was £2000, of which £300 was for the costs of planning, review and final evaluation meetings, £50 was for film, audio and video tapes for collecting evidence, and £250 was to pay an external evaluator to write an evaluation report. The total cost of planning and evaluation was £600, which represents 30% of the project budget.

Setting aims, objectives and measures of success

Evaluation cannot take place unless partners decide what it is they hope the project will achieve. One way of clarifying this is to agree:

- aims – the main purposes of a project, i.e. why a project is taking place. For example, an aim for a family literacy project might be 'to increase confidence and literacy skills in families with children under 5.'

- objectives – specific things partners want to achieve as a result of the project. You can think of objectives as steps towards the overall aims. Ideally, objectives should be SMART - Specific, Measurable, Achievable, Realistic, and within a Timescale - although arts objectives do not always readily fit this ideal. For example, an objective for the family literacy project might be 'to involve 10 families in a week-long creative event led by a storyteller and a poet at the local library.'

- measures of success – these show how you will know if an objective is achieved. They are also sometimes called performance indicators, success criteria or outcomes. In an arts education project, they are likely to be gains in skills, knowledge or understanding of the arts and creativity or personal or social change. For example a measure of success for the family literacy project might be increased use of the library by the participating families.

You should try to make clear links between your aims, objectives and measures of success. One way of doing this is to use a planning grid.

Tables 1 and 2 are planning grids with some examples of aims, objectives and measures of success for two partnership projects.

Table 1
Planning grid for a Youth Arts Project

A project involving a photographer, an artist using digital technology, a youth club and a primary care trust. Throughout the guide it is referred to as the Youth Arts Project. The grid focuses on an overarching aim for the project, and the objectives of two of the partners with linked measures of success.

Aims	Objectives	Measures of success
Why are we doing the project?	What specific things do we want to achieve?	How will we identify success
To promote healthy lifestyles among young people through a creative project	The primary care trust would like to: - increase young people's access to information about healthy lifestyles	Measures of success for the primary care trust would be - 80% of young people takin part attended a workshop led by a health promotion worker from the primary care trust - 80% of young people takin part produced a poster about teenage health issue
	Newtown Youth club would like to: - increase young people's self-esteem and confidence - give young people at Newtown Youth Club experience of working with professional artists	Measures of success for the youth club would be if - 80% of youth club membei completed the project

Aims	Objectives	Measures of success
Why are we doing the project?	What specific things do we want to achieve?	How will we identify success?
	- develop young people's creative skills	- all those completing the project could use digital cameras and Photoshop software - all those completing the project could make a range of portrait photographs and discuss them - at least half of those completing the project made digital images good enough to add to the youth.shire website
	- develop young people's awareness of media images	- young people showed increased understanding of the way body images are created in the media, and used appropriate language to analyse and discuss them

Table 2
Planning grid for a Primary School Music Theatre Project

This project involves a primary school, elderly people from a day centre, a musician, a visual artist, a dancer, and a local authority. Throughout the guide it is referred to as the Primary School Music Theatre Project. The grid focuses on an overarching aim for the project, and the objectives of two of the partners, with linked measures of success.

Aims	Objectives	Measures of success
Why are we doing the project?	What specific things do we want to achieve?	How will we identify success?
- To create positive relations between the school and other local institutions in the community	The school would like to: - increase the understanding of pupils in Years 5 and 6 of the needs of elderly people in the local community - establish permanent links with staff and elderly people at Sunny Bank Day Centre, based on taking part in creative activities	Measures of success for the school would be for: - pupils in Years 5 and 6 to show more positive attitudes towards elderly people in the community, during the project - two more joint arts projects to be set up between Sunny Bank and Jonston School over the next 24 months
	The day centre would like to: - introduce regular arts activities for visitors	A measure of success for the day centre would be if: - at least 5 elderly people who took part in the project asked for more arts activities

Managing the partnership

When all partners meet to decide on aims and objectives, they are likely to have many different agendas. It can be very difficult to get all partners to agree a set of aims, with objectives which can be realistically achieved through one project. It may well be that some aims and objectives will not be shared by all partners. Compromise is nearly always necessary. Try to:

- discuss all partners' agendas openly

- make sure you understand each other – you may think you are speaking the same language, but specialist terminology can be confusing

- focus on one or two overarching aims for the project, and encourage partners to express their different agendas through specific objectives

- focus on one or two overarching aims for the project, and encourage partners to express their different agendas through specific objectives

- agree objectives and measures of success which are *acceptable* to all, even if, they are not *shared* by all partners

- be realistic about what can be achieved

- be as specific as possible - what exactly are you trying to achieve?

- wherever possible, include participants in initial planning

For example, **Signals Media Arts** had a partnership-building and project development day for their *Cartoon Countryside* project. Partners filled in proformas with their own aims and objectives, which were then discussed with the group. Conflicts of interest between an environmental educationalist and the artists were exposed; the former wanted a high-quality end product, while the latter wanted to demystify the creative process. Compromise was reached when it was agreed that the artists would complete the post-production stage themselves to a high standard, but teachers and pupils would visit the artists at work.

Judging success and quality

It can be difficult to decide on measures of success for an arts project. The results of arts projects are unpredictable, and people's views on the quality of creative activity vary enormously. When setting measures of success, think about fitness for purpose and:

- the current levels of skills in, and knowledge and understanding of the arts and creativity, of those taking part

- realistic increases in skills, knowledge and understanding you might expect to see as a result of the project

- how you would define the current levels of personal and social development in relevant areas of the people taking part

- what kinds of changes in social and personal development you would hope to see

It may not be obvious immediately what people have learned or how they have changed as a result of a project. Try to be clear about what might be achieved:

- by the end of the project

- in the longer term

For example, in Going Places, a mental health outreach project run by Nottingham City Museums and Galleries Access Team, a short-term measure of success was for members of the group to produce a piece of work of which they were proud to display in the Castle Museum. A longer-term measure of success was for participants to visit museums in Nottingham, independently of the group and on a regular basis.

Unexpected outcomes

There are likely to be many unexpected outcomes, and these are as important as those for which you are planning. The interaction between an artist and a group of people is creative and dynamic, and often leads to outcomes no one has thought of. Well-planned evaluation can enable partners to notice, record and value the unexpected.

For example, Fabrica, a Brighton gallery which promotes understanding of contemporary art, set up a multimedia residency at Cardinal Newman School. The residency created an unexpectedly high level of interest from teachers, in a range of departments, who asked for an extra presentation after school about the creative use of multimedia technology. The enthusiasm of the young people taking part far exceeded expectations, with students working through break-times. Fabrica felt that both of these outcomes were strong measures of success.

Table 3 Possible measures of success

This table suggests some of the kinds of measures of success you might expect from an arts education project. The table concentrates on those taking part and group leaders. Other partners, such as arts organisations, will have different measures of success. You may only want to include a few from this list, or prefer to invent your own which relate to your aims and objectives.

During the project	
Arts and creative learning	The project creates opportunities for people taking part and group leaders to - engage in investigation, discovery and making which is new to them - learn new arts-based skills and techniques - have a creative experience which is new to them - engage in creative thinking - experience working with professional artists
Personal and social development	People taking part - enjoy themselves and feel confident - have opportunities to express their individuality - feel their creative contribution is valued - feel ownership of the project - show enthusiasm and commitment - co-operate with others - engage with issues and ideas which are important to them - engage with cultural difference
Other	The project generates - interest amongst people who are not taking part - a positive atmosphere and a 'buzz'

At the end of the project	
Arts and creative learning	People taking part - have increased their skills in, and knowledge and understanding of, creativity and of the artform(s) involved in the project - have made an artwork or taken part in a performance which is of higher quality than they have achieved before - have made an artwork or taken part in a performance that is judged of high quality by others Teachers and leaders - will be able to build on what they have learned in future arts and creative activities - have increased their skills in, and knowledge and understanding of, creativity and the artform(s) involved in the project
Personal and social development	The project resulted in - stronger teamwork - gains in confidence and self-esteem - increases in understanding of issues and ideas which are important to those taking part - greater understanding of cultural difference - solutions to community problems
Other	The project - had positive unexpected outcomes - strengthened links with outside communities

Longer-term outcomes	
Arts learning	The project - will be followed up in some way, or repeated for other groups - changes the way the arts are delivered - leads to creative approaches to delivering other activities - leads to further training in the arts and creative learning for group leaders - permanently raises expectations and standards in the arts
Personal and social development	The project - increases interest in the arts amongst those taking part, influencing leisure and career choices - contributes to permanent changes in the community
Other	- there is raised awareness of the impact of the arts among partners - partners feel confident about investing in arts projects - increased budgets are allocated to the arts by partners - partnership projects using the arts become embedded in thinking

Summary checklist for Stage 1 - Planning

- Who will have overall responsibility for evaluation?
- How much will evaluation cost in time and money?
- Have review sessions during and after the project been timetabled?
- What is the project's main aim, and its specific objectives and measures of success?
- Are they acceptable to all partners, including those taking part?
- Are they realistic?
- Do they take into account what might be achieved in the short and long term?
- How will unexpected outcomes be recognised and valued?

Stage 2 Collecting evidence

Focus questions for Stage 2
How will we collect the evidence we need?

Planning from the beginning

The last section helped partners think about setting aims, objectives and measures of success. This section helps you plan how to collect evidence about your activity which will be useful for evaluation. You need to decide at the planning stages how and when to gather evidence.

When to collect evidence

You need to collect evidence before, during and at the end of a project. Evidence collected before the project begins shows the level of skills, knowledge and understanding, or personal and social development, of people who will take part in the project. Without knowing this base line, it is difficult to show what has changed as a result of the project.

Often people forget to collect evidence until a project is over. If you do this, you will not have a clear picture of what happened at each stage, nor will you be able to review the project's progress and make adjustments if necessary.

For example, Action Factory Community Arts designed a simple preparatory survey sheet for young people to complete before taking part in the project, *Careers Education through Participative Arts.* The sheet asked the young people about any arts activities they did already, how often they did them, and what ideas they had for careers. To test out understanding of careers in the arts, a list of jobs was included, and pupils were asked to tick which jobs could be seen as working in the arts.

Documenting the project

When planning, partners may also need to consider how the project is going to be documented. Documentation means keeping a record of what happens during the project. For example, a partner may keep records of the project through minutes of meetings, programmes, photographs, funding applications and contracts with freelance artists.

Documentation is not the same as evaluation, although it may contribute to evaluation. For evaluation, it is likely that you will need to collect more specific information, using techniques which are additional to routine documentation.

Monitoring

Monitoring is also different from evaluation, although evidence collected through monitoring may, like documentation, contribute to evaluation. The term 'monitoring' is used in different contexts. For example, security procedures may be monitored regularly to check fire exits are clear or that money is collected efficiently and safely. Monitoring can also describe routine collection of data, such as attendance figures, or checking of materials and equipment to make sure they are of good quality.

Some of the data you collect through monitoring may be used in evaluation. However, when you plan evaluation you need to decide what evidence will be most useful, and whether or not additional or different data will be needed to find out if you have achieved the specific objectives of the project you are evaluating.

What kinds of evidence?

The evidence you collect is to help you judge if you have achieved the aims and objectives set during planning, and any unplanned outcomes, and is not just for keeping a record. It is likely that two kinds of evidence will be needed by partners to show what has been achieved, quantitative and qualitative evidence.

● Quantitative evidence produces data which enables you to measure numbers or percentages and statistics. It tends to deal with facts, such as the number of people taking part, or the cost per head of the project.

● Qualitative evidence shows people's thoughts, opinions, ideas and feelings. Qualitative evidence may be more difficult to interpret, but is important for the evaluation of arts activities. Most usefully, qualitative information is collected from people with different points of views, who bring different perspectives.

Qualitative evidence
● gives a sense of what really happened
● allows judgement of the quality of the project
● shows if and how people changed through the creative process
● is likely to reveal unexpected outcomes

In a partnership project, partners should aim to collect a combination of quantitative and qualitative evidence. Sometimes funding can be dependent on quantitative evidence, such as certain levels of attendance or participation. Check what is needed during planning.

For example, 54 children from Year 3 at Cavendish First School worked with 2 artists over 6 days on *Inside Me,* an animation project about expressing feelings. These facts are quantitative evidence. The video of the finished animated film and the thoughts and ideas of some of the children about how they were now better able to express their feelings, also captured on video, are qualitative evidence. The video also included comments from a teacher about how the children had developed emotional literacy, giving another perspective and strengthening the qualitative evidence of change.

Choosing ways of collecting evidence

To help choose the right methods of collecting evidence for your project, ask yourself the following questions.

- Will the methods give us the evidence we need, including funders' requirements?
- Are they flexible enough to reveal unexpected outcomes?
- Are the methods 'user friendly' for everyone taking part?
- Do they take account of equal opportunities, ethical and safeguarding issues for children, young people and vulnerable adults?
- Has everyone agreed how evidence will be used and if it will be attributed to individuals?
- Will evidence be collected from a wide range and number of people taking part?
- Will evidence be likely to give different points of view?
- Can evidence be collected without disrupting the project, perhaps as part of a daily routine?
- Do we have the resources to manage the methods we have chosen?

Safeguarding issues about collecting evidence from children, young people and vulnerable adults are discussed in another Arts Council England publication, *Keeping Arts Safe*, (see Appendix 6). You should be particularly aware that you need to get permission from authorised carers before taking photographs or video recordings of children, young people and vulnerable adults. It is also good practice to seek consent before asking children to complete questionnaires. Ethical issues about gathering evidence from disadvantaged groups are discussed in Moriarty's *Sharing practice: a guide to self-evaluation in the context of social exclusion* (see Appendix 6).

If you are planning to collect personal information about individuals, you will need to make sure that you work within the Data Protection Act 1998. You may need to apply for a licence if you are going to use personal information such as people's names and addresses. Information on data protection can be found at www.informationcommissioner.gov.uk or telephone the helpline on 01625 545 745.

Techniques for collecting evidence

There are many ways of collecting evidence, such as:

- comments' boxes and books
- displays of work or performance at the end of a project
- drawings, charts and diagrams
- 'graffiti' walls
- interviews
- observation
- online websites, chatrooms and email
- participatory techniques
- photography
- questionnaires
- small group discussions
- tape recordings
- video recordings
- written diaries

Appendix 3 on page 52 gives more information about each of these techniques, and examples of using them.

No one method is perfect and you could consider a variety of approaches to make sure you get the quantitative and qualitative information you need. Try not always to fall back on the methods most familiar to you, but think carefully about the best technique to gather the evidence you need. Table 4 summarises the advantages and disadvantages of each technique. The list of techniques is not meant to be exhaustive, but to give you some starting points.

Table 5 on page 29 gives examples of how evidence could be collected in the Youth Arts Project and the Primary School Music Theatre Project.

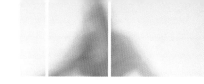

Table 4 Advantages and disadvantages of some methods of collecting evidence

Method	Advantages	Disadvantages
Comments' box and book	- Simple and cheap - Easy to organise during and after a project - Comments can be anonymous, and this may help people to be honest	- Comments may be very wide-ranging, and it might be difficult to draw clear conclusions - Reliant on literacy skills
Display or performance at end of project	- An opportunity to share and celebrate what has been achieved - Attractive evidence to funders and others	- In participatory projects, end-products can be disappointing, even though the process of getting to the end has been excellent - Some people may have unrealistic expectations of the quality of the final product - Show the result, not the process
Drawings, charts and diagrams	- Drawings and diagrams are a simple and cheap way of recording expectations and charting change - Not reliant on literacy skills	- Some people find drawing intimidating - May give only limited insights into views and experiences
'Graffiti' wall	- Simple, cheap and fun - Informal and likely to engage young people - Useful at events such as conferences, where people can add comments as they pass by	- Others can read the comments. This can lead to copying and peer-group pressure. - A mass of comments can be difficult to disentangle and interpret - Reliant on literacy skills

Method	Advantages	Disadvantages
Individual interviews	- Allow in-depth discussion of a range of questions - Can be conducted in private	- Time-consuming to carry out more than a handful of interviews, so evidence may be seen as limited and unconvincing - Some people may feel intimidated - Interviewer may influence or 'lead' responses
Observation	- Tried and tested technique of following the progress of a small number of people experiencing an activity - Can give in-depth insight into people's experiences and interest - Good for gaining insight into the experience as a whole, and for evaluating management and workshop skills	- Time-consuming and labour intensive - People may find it intrusive - Difficult to observe a group systematically, but following one or two people through a session or visit can be illuminating
Online websites, chat rooms and email	- Quick, easy and interactive method of collecting comments from a wide range of people - Useful for collecting evidence during a project and maintaining communication - Likely to appeal to young people	- Can be difficult to ensure target audiences know about online sites - Time-consuming and expensive to maintain content and analyse comments - Internet access and activities need to be kept safe for children, young people and vulnerable adults
Participatory techniques	- Enjoyable way of finding out views and feelings - Can create a positive atmosphere and help with teambuilding - Not reliant on literacy skills	- Need specialist drama-based skills, or a confident non-specialist - Can be intimidating for some people - Evidence gained may be difficult to interpret

Method	Advantages	Disadvantages
Photography	- Digital cameras are easy to use and give instant access to images for sharing and editing - People taking part can take their own photographs, as artists and leaders - Provides documentation as well as evidence for evaluation - Not dependent on literacy skills	- Difficult to decide who or what to photograph to ensure evidence is useful and convincing - Danger of ending up with a huge amount of descriptive material which is difficult to interpret - Can be difficult to get permission to use images of children, young people and vulnerable adults to avoid potential misuse of images, especially online. This is best done in advance
Questionnaires	- Can be completed in private and returned by post or filled in at an event or activity - Large numbers can be distributed - Can be simple tick box/agree/disagree in style, or ask more open questions	- Often not completed or returned unless filled in at the event or activity - Sometimes reveal superficial information, rather than in-depth views - Rely on literacy skills, which may be inappropriate for some people - The questions may define the responses if not carefully constructed
Small group discussions (focus groups)	- Can be a secure setting to get a range of opinions - Structured discussion can set off wide-ranging views and feedback	- Can be difficult to arrange in some settings - May not be a typical group, as only the most confident may take part or contribute - Group dynamics can be difficult to overcome - Ideally, two people needed to run the group - one to take notes and one to facilitate

Method	Advantages	Disadvantages
Tape Recordings	- Cheap and easy to manage - Can be operated by participants - Not dependent on literacy skills - Support other methods of collecting evidence, such as interviews and focus groups	- Danger of ending up with a huge amount of descriptive material which is time-consuming to transcribe
Video	- A flexible medium, which is relatively easy to manage - Digital recordings available instantly for sharing and editing - Likely to appeal to young people, who may enjoy operating the equipment themselves - Not dependent on literacy skills	- Can be intrusive in a small space - Danger of ending up with a huge amount of unedited material which is difficult to interpret - Equipment can be expensive - People may 'perform' for the camera - Can be difficult to get permission to use images of children, young people and vulnerable adults to avoid potential misuse of images, especially online. This is best done in advance
Written diary	- With a clear structure can provide documentation and evidence of change during activities for artists and participants - Simple and cheap	- Relies on literacy skills - Diaries may be seen as private, and participants or artists may be unwilling to share contents - Participants may present a falsely positive view

Table 5 Collecting evidence

The Youth Arts Project

This table shows possible ways of collecting evidence for three measures of success in the Youth Arts Project in Table 1

Measures of success	Ways of collecting evidence
- 80% of youth club members complete project	- Attendance register
- All those completing the project can use digital cameras and Photoshop software	- 5 participants asked to answer 4 or 5 questions on video before, during and at the end of the project, as a video diary - Examples of photographs and digital images made by young people
- Young people show increased understanding of the way body images are created in the media, and use appropriate language to analyse and discuss them	- Small group discussion at beginning, middle and end of the project

The Primary School Music Theatre Project

This table shows possible ways of collecting evidence for one of the
measures of success in the Primary School Music Theatre Project in Table 2

Measures of success	Ways of collecting evidence
- Pupils in Years 5 and 6 show more positive attitudes towards elderly people in the community, during the project	- Time-lapse photography during the project of a small group of pupils, focusing on facial expression and body language - Interviews with 3 pupils from the group before, during and at the end of the project - Interviews with 3 elderly people before, during and at the end of the project

Summary checklist for Stage 2 - Collecting Evidence

- Will evidence be collected before, during and at the end of the project?

- How will the project be documented?

- Will the evidence collected reveal what all the partners need to know?

- Are the methods of collecting evidence flexible enough to reveal unexpected outcomes?

- Will the evidence show a range of viewpoints?

- How will people taking part be asked what they think of the project?

- Do the methods for collecting evidence take account of equal opportunities, ethical and safeguarding issues?

- Are the methods manageable?

- Has the use of evidence been agreed with those providing it?

Stage 3 Assembling and interpreting

Focus questions for Stage 3

What does the evidence tell us?

When to assemble and interpret the evidence

This section helps you bring together and interpret the evidence you have collected. It also suggests when to assemble and interpret the evidence:

- for a review meeting while the project is in progress

- after the project has ended

What does the evidence tell us?

Until it is interpreted, evidence may not tell you very much. You need to turn raw data into information. Information can help partners to draw conclusions and take action if necessary. Interpreting evidence can be a difficult task, and you need to allow enough time for it. For example, reading 30 questionnaires and comparing and summarising the answers to 6 questions can take several hours.

For example, in the Youth Arts Project the number of young people attending sessions – let's say 16 – is data. Turning this number into a percentage – 80% of the possible membership of 20, and then making a comparison with attendance at other sessions – is information. Normally about 13 or 14 young people attend. During the arts project 16 have attended regularly, so there has been an increase of 10%.

The video diaries of young people responding to questions provide raw qualitative evidence. By watching the tapes once or twice you could draw out two or three points which keep recurring. This turns the evidence into information which will help you see if you have achieved your measures of success.

Using percentages

When turning some data into information you are likely to use percentages. If you do, you should always explain how many or how much would be 100%. 7 out of 10 people or 70 people out of 100 are both 70%. However, evidence based on what 70 people say, as opposed to what 7 people say may carry more weight. It is important that the basis of the information you are offering is clear. Generally, it is good practice to note your sample size (the number of people who provided data) and explain how the data was gathered.

Interpreting qualitative evidence

Qualitative evidence gathered for example from interviews, group discussions or a final performance may not be as easy to interpret as quantitative data. You may have collected a wide range of very different opinions, especially about the quality of the creative process and outcomes, and find it difficult to draw conclusions. The following techniques may help you.

- Look back at your original measures of success to help pick out what you need.

- Avoid being unduly influenced by a tiny number of either very positive or very critical comments.

- Try to establish the majority view.

- Check that your judgements are based on evidence from different categories of people involved with the project (e.g. participants, artists, group leaders).

- Initially sort comments into positive and negative groups.

- Focus on evidence which shows change, progress and development.

- Look for unexpected outcomes.

For example, a teacher at Farnborough Comprehensive School judged the quality of a workshop on Shakespeare texts by Reckless Sleepers, an experimental theatre company and visual art group, by:

- using his knowledge of the students' previous achievement
- observing the students during the session and noting how they developed their creative thinking and their confidence in using the techniques of physical theatre, which were new to them
- listening to students' comments at a post-workshop discussion, many of which showed how their attitudes to Shakespeare had changed and become more positive

---

Combining different kinds of evidence

Your evidence is likely to include many 'quotable quotes'. Used alone these may give a flavour of the project, and can often sum up unexpected outcomes, but they will be most convincing if you can provide some quantitative evidence and analysis to support them.

For example, Chichester Festival Theatre analysed the responses from parents to a questionnaire about a summer school. Each question used a combination of scoring and opportunities for open comment. In the analysis, the comments were given a context through the quantitative information.

Question: What did you think of the activities the children participated in during the week?

Scoring: 88% thought that the activities were good, and gave them 5/5.

Comments included:

- *Great - the first day she wasn't sure but soon got into all the activities.*
- *He loved it all. After the first day he said, 'Can I do this next year?'*
- *Couldn't stop talking about everything they'd done.*

Why have a review meeting?

Reviewing a short workshop can be as informal as the artist stopping for five minutes to check that people taking part and the group leader are happy with what is happening. During a longer project, a more formal review meeting gives everyone a chance to take stock of how things are progressing and to voice their views. Action can be taken to adjust the project if necessary. As many partners as possible, including some people taking part, should attend the review meeting during the project. There is more chance of this happening if arrangements for the review meeting are made during the early planning stages.

Running a review meeting during the project

A project review meeting could:

- update partners on what has happened
- share what the evidence suggests so far
- decide on necessary actions

It will be far easier to have a short, effective meeting if as much interpretation of the evidence as possible has been done before the meeting.

Table 6

Reviewing evidence collected during the first stage of the Youth Arts Project

This table shows how some of the evidence collected by the fourth week of the project could be presented at a review meeting for discussion and used to make adjustments to the project.

Source of evidence	What we found out	Action to be taken
- Attendance register	- Attendance at 80%: 10% higher than usual	- None
- 5 participants asked to answer 5 questions on video	- 3 participants have learned new camera skills; 2 felt that they have learned no new skills, and were quite bored in some of the camera sessions - Using Photoshop is the most popular activity	- Discussion with photographer about making the camera-work more challenging for some young people - Consider increasing input from digital artist
- Examples of photographs and digital images made so far	- High quality photographs and digital images are being produced	- None
- Small group discussion at beginning and middle of project	- Young people have been challenged by the discussion of body image and are thinking deeply about media images	- None

Making changes

Reviewing the evidence may lead to taking action, including:

- changing the day-to-day organisation of the project
- changing the creative activity
- resetting measures of success
- adjusting objectives

For example, after a review meeting of a multimedia residency, set up by Fabrica Gallery, all partners decided:

- that there was not enough equipment, and that the structure of sessions needed to be changed
- to stop using a large touch-screen, because it was not relevant to the work of the group
- to change one of the objectives, which had been to use the theme of Fabrica's summer show, and give the students a chance to work to a personal brief
- to exhibit the work produced by the students at the school. This was an unexpected outcome and a measure of the project's success
- to extend the timetable to allow the students to finish the project with the artist

---

Meeting after the project

You can structure a meeting to evaluate the project when it is over on the same lines as the review meeting. All partners should be present, including some people who took part, if possible. The main purpose of the meeting is to decide whether or not the project was successful. Did it achieve the original or adjusted objectives you set? Many unexpected outcomes will have emerged, and these will need to be recognised and discussed. At the meeting:

- begin by looking at the documentation, to update everyone about the project
- keep documentation brief. A display of photographs, or short video extracts, with a chart or timetable listing the main activities may be enough
- organise evidence as at the review meeting. Aim to interpret evidence and transform data into information
- remind partners of the project's aim(s) and objectives

Table 7
Presenting evidence collected at the end of a project:
the Primary School Music Theatre Project

Suggested way of presenting evidence for a meeting of partners at the end of the Primary School Music Theatre Project. The table focuses on one of the school's objectives about increasing empathy between pupils and elderly people. You could also include the project's aim on the table, or present it separately.

What specific things did we want to achieve?	Measures of success	What did we find out?	Were the aims and objectives achieved? Any unexpected outcomes?
- to increase the understanding of pupils in Years 5 and 6 of the needs of elderly people in the local community	- pupils in Years 5 and 6 show more positive attitudes towards elderly people in the community, during the project	- an increase in friendly talk between old and young, and more relaxed and happy facial expressions as the project progressed - 2 of the 3 children interviewed said that they liked elderly people more now - elderly people felt the children communicated better with them as the project went on, and enjoyed working with them	- Yes – the project definitely contributed to the aim of creating good relations within the community - Years 5 and 6 have greatly increased their understanding of local elderly people - an unexpected outcome is that five Year 6 pupils have started calling in to the day centre after school as volunteer helpers

Getting an overview

You may have a lot of evidence to present, especially if there were many measures of success. It may now be useful to try to bring together all the information, and get an overview of the project. SWOT analysis, the listing of Strengths, Weaknesses, Opportunities and Threats, is one helpful way to order a lot of information and begin to draw out the lessons to be learned from the project. It provides a context for reviewing what did not work so well, and shows areas for improvement (see Stage 4 for more detail).

Think of :

● strengths and weaknesses as good and disappointing points about the project itself

● opportunities and threats as good and bad things outside the project, which could affect future partnership projects

An active way of going about a SWOT listing is to use a flip chart and a brain-storming approach, and to ask all those at the evaluation meeting to take part. This could be done after the presentation of the evidence. Alternatively, the SWOT could be prepared in advance, and partners asked to comment.

Table 8
Presenting information in a SWOT analysis

Part of the Strengths, Weaknesses, Opportunities and Threats listing
for the Primary School Music Theatre Project.

Strengths	Weaknesses
- An ambitious project with many partners - The aims of all partners were met and there were positive unexpected outcomes - Project created great enthusiasm and excitement among pupils in Years 5 and 6, including many who had not enjoyed taking part in other school performances - Project generated interest in arts for health and social purposes among day centre residents and workers	- Audience for the final performance was disappointing - Project disturbed other activities at school, and demanded far more teacher time than planned - Costs underestimated – more funding needed for props, scenery and other materials - Transport for the elderly people to the school proved difficult and unreliable
Opportunities	**Threats**
- The project could be promoted as a regional and possibly a national model - Could extend the relationship between Sunny Bank and Jonston Primary School through other curriculum areas and through the After School Club - The local authority could explore further the creative needs of elderly people	- Funding for future partnership projects – not clear where this will come from, so how will we build on the success of this project? - Pressure on time due to national testing threatens this kind of project in primary schools

Summary checklist for Stage 3 - Assembling and interpreting

- Has data been changed into information?
- Has the information been interpreted in advance for presentation at evaluation meetings, during and at the end of the project?
- Does the presentation show if aims and objectives have been achieved?
- Have unexpected outcomes been included?
- Has descriptive documentation been kept to a minimum?
- Has the information been put together to give an overview of the project?

Stage 4 Reflecting and moving forward

Focus questions for Stage 4

What have we learned from the evaluation?
How will we do things differently in future?

Learning from evaluation

A meeting at the end of the project should not be the end of the evaluation process. Partners need to reflect on the evaluation, to make sure that what was learned is used to improve future practice. This section is about how to move on positively and constructively after evaluation.

How and when to reflect

Some partnerships may have completed one of a series of projects, and be preparing to work together again. If this is the case, reflecting and moving forward may best be approached as a group, and findings fed into the next project.

Other partnerships may be unlikely to link up in the same combination for another arts project. If so, reflecting and moving forward may be a way for each partner to think separately about what they have learned from the evaluation, and how this will affect the way they approach partnership arts projects in the future. This might be done at an internal meeting after the project, or at an annual review meeting to discuss wider issues.

The following questions may help partnerships and partners reflect on the project and the findings of the evaluation.

● What were the key findings from the evaluation for the partnership or for individual partners?

● If a SWOT analysis was done, were there particular strengths, weaknesses, opportunities or threats which need to be considered?

● How can strengths and opportunities be built on?

● How can weaknesses be reduced, and threats be overcome?

● Is the project likely to have longer-term outcomes, as yet unknown? If so, how will partners find out about them? Are they likely to be significant for future work?

For example, after the evaluation of the *Oklahoma Dance Project* the Head of Arts Education at John Masefield High School concluded that:

- a similar project should become an annual event

- it should include all feeder schools

- it should increase from 3 to 5 days

- the local community should be more involved in the project

- there should be a single day of the project for boys only

- the local youth dance worker should be involved

- open rehearsals should take place both in and out of school time

Comparing projects

Evaluating one arts partnership project can help you to make changes and do things better next time. If you have evaluated several projects, comparing what you found out from each will give you a strong basis on which to make decisions.

When reflecting, ask yourself these questions:

- How successful was the most recent project compared with other, similar projects?

- Does the comparison tell us anything about future work in this area?

For example, Hartlepool Borough Council Community Services compared two dance access projects and realised that more people had dropped out of the second project. The evaluation showed that people had found the style and approach of the second project more difficult. Officers concluded that the project leader must be given a clear understanding of community needs in advance to ensure a successful access project. Ongoing communication between the project leader and people taking part is also vital for future projects.

Moving forward

Reflecting on what has been learned from one or more projects might help:

- an arts organisation to make changes to the way they plan partnership projects, after noting that partners often have different expectations of what projects can achieve

- an individual artist to decide that she or he works best with adults

- a youth group to allocate more funding to arts projects because they consistently increase attendance

- a school to make changes to the way the arts curriculum is delivered

However or whenever it takes place, reflecting and moving forward is a vital part of using evaluation to improve practice and strengthen decision-making.

For example, after evaluating *The Vision,* a digital arts initiative for schools, Arts Access concluded that early planning meetings did not spend enough time on clarifying aims, objectives and measures of success, with the result that partners did not always share a common approach to the project. Arts Access's projects in the future will probably involve multiple partnerships, and it will become increasingly important for all partners to understand and agree to shared aims and objectives.

Summary checklist for Stage 4 - Reflecting and moving forward

- How will partners reflect on the evaluation?

- What were the key findings from the evaluation?

- How did the project compare with others?

- What decisions and changes should now be made?

Stage 5 Reporting and sharing

Focus questions for Stage 5

Who will we tell about the project and why?

How will we tell them?

What will we tell them?

Using the evaluation to show what happened

Reflecting on the findings of the evaluation is important for improving practice, as we discussed in Stage 4. The other main purpose of evaluation is to show what happened as a result of a project. This section suggests ways of sharing the findings of your evaluation with partners and others.

By following Stages 1 to 4 of this Guide, you should be able to get together whatever is required by any partner. This may range from completing a simple form to providing a full project report. Remember that people taking part also need to know about the findings of the evaluation.

Telling people outside the partnership

Before sharing any information from the evaluation, especially with anyone outside the partnership, make sure that all partners, including people taking part, agree to it. This is especially important if you are working with disadvantaged groups, who can easily feel powerless in the context of evaluation or research. It is also important where information is not anonymous, or if any group or individual is criticised in the evaluation.

You should also be aware of the safeguarding issues for children, young people and vulnerable adults in using photography, digital images or video recordings in printed material and on the internet. Parents or carers must give consent and agree the specific use of images. You should ensure that the names of children and young people cannot be linked to images which are going to be used, and any identifiable marks (birthmarks, tattoos) are not shown. These issues are discussed further in *Keeping Arts Safe*, Arts Council England, 2003 (see Appendix 6).

Thinking about the points that emerged from a SWOT analysis is one way of deciding who to tell about the project beyond the partnership. Try to be clear about what different people need to know. There is no need to tell people everything you have found out.

For example, all three partners opted for different ways to share the outcomes of the animation project, *Inside Me.*

- Cavendish First School made a large folder, with copies of the children's drawings and writing, as a long-term school resource, and displayed it in the school entrance hall for parents, governors and children.

- Artworks cut a second video, with press coverage and evaluative comments from the children about their thoughts on the project added to the animation.

- The Artists in Schools Co-ordinator wrote an article for the Bradford Education News about the project, and presented a report to the LEA management team and elected members.

Ways of reporting

While written reports can be useful, they are not the only way of telling people about a project. Other ways of reporting may be more appropriate for some people, and may capture more closely what the project was about. However, approaches to sharing findings which are not based on written reports can become similar to documentation. They may provide a description and celebration of the project, without including any judgements or conclusions from the evaluation.

For example, young people who took part in the film project *Kicking Arts* on the Isle of Wight invited funders, parents and friends to see the completed film at their youth club. As part of the project, the young people had written reports about their own views on whether or not the project had fulfilled its aims and objectives. These reports were displayed for guests to read at the launch.

Writing a project report

A clear advantage of a written project report is that it provides a permanent record. This may be useful for:

● building up an archive to save 're-inventing the wheel' for another project

● sharing ideas and good practice with others

● helping with future funding applications

● showing people what you do

If you follow the steps in this Guide through each stage, it should reduce the burden of writing a report. By now you will have collected most of the material needed.

Common pitfalls of written reports

The most common weakness of project reports is that they include too much description and not enough analysis, conclusions and action points. To try to overcome this problem:

● aim to make your report as short as possible

● avoid long, unbroken passages of text

● use tables and bullet points to summarise

● remember that photographs and diagrams save on words

Keep asking these questions:

● Are we just telling the story of the project?

● Have we interpreted the evidence?

● Have we made judgements based on the evidence and drawn conclusions?

Table 9
Suggested format for a written evaluation report

This table suggests some section headings for a report and gives
ideas about what to include in each section.

Section heading	Stage	Suggested content
Context	*Stage 1*	• Why the partnership came together • The setting for the project • Basic data about the people taking part • When the project took place and the timetable • How and why the artist/arts organisation was selected • Thanks – especially to funders and helpers
Description of project	*Stages 2 and 3*	• A summary of what happened • Include some documentation, such as photos of examples of work, programmes, audience figures and press cuttings as appendices
Aims, objectives and measures of success	*Stages 1 and 2*	• Aims, objectives and measures of success as agreed during planning with changes made after the review meeting • Explain how you evaluated the project • Include examples such as questionnaire formats or questions used in interviews in the appendices
What we found out	*Stage 3*	• What the evidence told you • If aims and objectives were achieved • A summary of the success or otherwise of the project • Unexpected outcomes • Include details of evidence collected and its interpretation in appendices
Overview of the project	*Stage 3*	• A SWOT analysis or other overview

Section heading	Stage	Suggested content
Lessons learned from the evaluation	*Stages 4 and 5*	• Conclusions: a summary of what lessons have been learned • How these will change what happens in future • How people have been told about the project so far
Appendices		Might include: - CV of artist or description of arts organisation - Project brief for artist/arts organisation - Examples of questionnaires and interview formats - Details of evidence collected and its interpretation - Programmes, audience figures - Press cuttings - Examples of work, or photographs of work - Budget

Summary checklist for Stage 5 – Reporting and sharing

- What methods of reporting are needed, which will satisfy all partners?
- Will these take account of safeguarding, ethical and confidentiality issues?
- How have the findings of the evaluation been shared with people who took part?
- Who else should be told about the project?
- What do they need to know?
- What would be the best way of recording the project and presenting the findings of the evaluation?

Summary checklist

Stage 1 – Planning

- [ ] Who will have overall responsibility for evaluation?
- [ ] How much will evaluation cost in time and money?
- [ ] Have review sessions during and after the project been timetabled?
- [ ] What is the project's main aim, and its objectives and measures of success?
- [ ] Are they acceptable to all partners, including those taking part?
- [ ] Are they realistic?
- [ ] Do they take into account what might be achieved in the short and long term?
- [ ] How will unexpected outcomes be recognised and valued?

Stage 2 – Collecting evidence

- [ ] Will evidence be collected before, during and at the end of the project?
- [ ] How will the project be documented?
- [ ] Will the evidence collected reveal what all the partners need to know?
- [ ] Are the methods of collecting evidence flexible enough to reveal unexpected outcomes?
- [ ] Will the evidence show a range of viewpoints?
- [ ] How will people taking part be asked what they think of the project?
- [ ] Do the methods for collecting evidence take account of equal opportunities, ethical and safeguarding issues?
- [ ] Are the methods manageable?
- [ ] Has the use of evidence been agreed with those providing it?

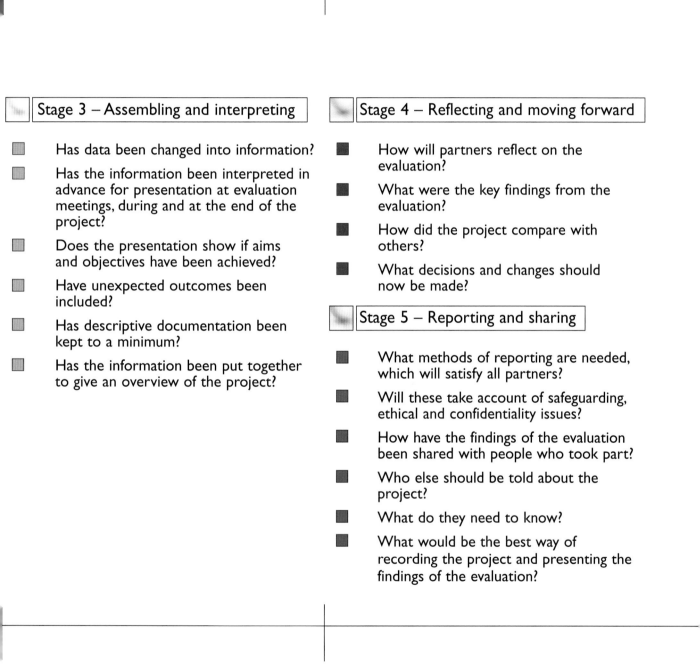

Stage 3 – Assembling and interpreting

- ☐ Has data been changed into information?
- ☐ Has the information been interpreted in advance for presentation at evaluation meetings, during and at the end of the project?
- ☐ Does the presentation show if aims and objectives have been achieved?
- ☐ Have unexpected outcomes been included?
- ☐ Has descriptive documentation been kept to a minimum?
- ☐ Has the information been put together to give an overview of the project?

Stage 4 – Reflecting and moving forward

- ☐ How will partners reflect on the evaluation?
- ☐ What were the key findings from the evaluation?
- ☐ How did the project compare with others?
- ☐ What decisions and changes should now be made?

Stage 5 – Reporting and sharing

- ☐ What methods of reporting are needed, which will satisfy all partners?
- ☐ Will these take account of safeguarding, ethical and confidentiality issues?
- ☐ How have the findings of the evaluation been shared with people who took part?
- ☐ Who else should be told about the project?
- ☐ What do they need to know?
- ☐ What would be the best way of recording the project and presenting the findings of the evaluation?

Appendix I

Setting standards for evaluation: self-review

You may find it useful to consider the table below, for a quick reference guide to your current practice in evaluation.

Where would you place your practice in evaluation as a partner or as a partnership on the table below? Use one or two recent projects as examples to help you decide. This may help you choose which of the five stages in the Guide will be most useful to you when you are doing evaluation.

Level 1 – emerging	Self-review
We are aware of the importance of evaluation and usually get some feedback. We sometimes report on a project, especially if asked to by a funder, although we tend to end up with a lot of description. Evaluation probably helps us improve projects, but we are not quite sure how to feed back findings into future projects.	
Level 2 – established	**Self-review**
We discuss evaluation at the planning stages of a project, and decide how to collect the views of those taking part and other partners. We sometimes find it difficult to put together and interpret the evidence we have collected, although we report on projects if asked to by funding partners. We usually meet partners at the end to share ideas about what worked well, and what we need to do better next time.	
Level 3 – advanced	**Self-review**
Evaluation is integral to our practice. We use a variety of methods to document projects and collect evidence. We ensure that all partners are involved in evaluation, including people taking part. We review projects as they progress, and interpret the evidence we collect at the end of the project. We report on projects in ways which are appropriate for different partners, and try to consider how to evaluate longer-term outcomes. Evaluation helps us make decisions and deliver higher-quality arts projects.	

Appendix 2
External and internal evaluation:
advantages and disadvantages

The Guide focuses on helping partners to evaluate their own projects, but there may be circumstances when you would find it better to organise external evaluation of a project. Even with an external evaluation, partners should ensure that they are fully involved with the process.

External evaluation	
Advantages	*Disadvantages*
- Time is allocated to the evaluation because it is paid for - Could be seen as more objective by people outside, and so the conclusions may be more credible - May bring in new perspectives, widen discussion and increase learning for partners - More likely to raise questions some partners will hesitate to bring up if evaluation is internal	- Likely to add considerably to project costs - Partners have less control over the evaluation process and may have less ownership of it - The process may be less integral to the project and 'bolted on' - Exposing difficult issues and weaknesses may alienate some partners

Internal evaluation	
Advantages	*Disadvantages*
- Probably cheaper in cash terms - Creates ownership, which is more likely to lead to reflection and changes in practice - The partnership can both control the process and suit it to their needs - Partners can avoid going too far with critical comments	- Takes considerable time and is likely to be an additional task for one or more partners - May lack credibility with outsiders - The evaluation may be narrower, without an external perspective - More likely to skirt round difficult issues or weaknesses

Appendix 3
Techniques for collecting evidence

Comments' box or book

You can place a set of blank postcards beside a box, and ask people to jot down their comments on a postcard during or after your activity and 'post' it in the box. The responses should give you a sense of how things are going, and may indicate particular issues which need to be discussed in more detail and resolved during or after the activity.

A comments' book at an exhibition or in a theatre foyer allows audiences to give an instant reaction to their experience. It can give you a sense of how your exhibition or performance was received, and may prompt you to make minor changes if appropriate.

> *For example,* Cavendish First School asked guests to write in a visitors' book at the launch of the video of their animation project, *Inside Me*. Comments were collected from elected members, inspectors, parents, governors and others.

Display or performance at end of project

What is made or performed at the end of the project is an important source of evidence for evaluation. You may need to provide a commentary for visitors or audiences explaining the background to and process of the project. Ask yourself these questions.

- How will the audience, people taking part and others have a chance to give feedback on the quality of the final product?
- How can we document the final performance as part of the project?
- How will the audience or visitors understand enough of the process of the project when they see the final product?

Drawings, charts and diagrams

You can use bar charts and pie diagrams, to show how much time or importance will be given to different activities, and to present information in an easily digestible form. Timetables are useful to make sure everyone knows what they are supposed to be doing, and also for checking progress during the project. Sometimes people, especially children, are more willing or able to draw their feelings about something, than to write about it. Pairs of drawings can be used to show how people would like things to change as a result of the project. You can revisit the drawings at the end of the project, to see if these ambitions have been met or have changed. Groups can design posters or leaflets to show the best things about a project.

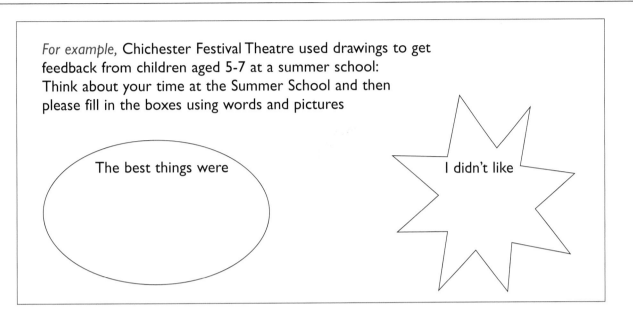

For example, Chichester Festival Theatre used drawings to get
feedback from children aged 5-7 at a summer school:
Think about your time at the Summer School and then
please fill in the boxes using words and pictures

The best things were

I didn't like

'Graffiti' walls

This is a more public version of a comments' box. Anyone involved with the project
can write a comment on a large sheet of paper fixed to the wall or on the floor.
To give some structure to the exercise, you can ask for comments on a particular
aspect of the project.

Individual interviews

One-to-one interviews are good for getting detailed qualitative evidence of opinions,
feelings and ideas. Plan your questions in advance. You will need a combination of
questions which you ask everyone, and some which vary, depending on what role
the person being interviewed had in your activity. It is easier to draw conclusions
when different kinds of people (e.g. participants, funders, artists, group leaders) have
been asked some similar questions. Some interviews are 'semi-structured', with
fewer prepared questions. This approach allows the person answering to talk about
things more freely.

For example, artists taking part in the Hall i'th' Wood Arts Project organised by
Bolton, Bury and Rochdale Artists in Schools, were interviewed and asked:

What were your expectations of the project when you were first approached?

How were these realised?

How could the activity have been structured to maximise co-operative working
between the artist, teachers and students?

What strengths did the project have?

What were its weaknesses?

How could it be improved in the future?

When setting up interviews:

- make sure you have a quiet, private area and enough time available

- explain to the person being interviewed what questions you will ask, how long it will take (set a time limit), and agree with them how their comments will be used

- be prepared to hear both positive and negative feedback

- listen rather than lead

- think ahead about how you will keep a record of what is said. Notes under each question are simplest

- taped interviews are very time-consuming to transcribe, but mean that you have a complete record of the interview. A taped conversation also gives you the precise words people used, which can be very powerful. You should ask for permission before taping an interview, and explain how the tape will be used

- you should avoid one-to-one interviews with children, young people and vulnerable adults because of the safeguarding issues, unless a carer or authorised adult is present. One solution is to ask a carer or authorised leader to carry out and record an interview for you, based on questions which you provide. See the guide *Keeping Arts Safe* published by Arts Council England for more advice and information (see Appendix 6).

Observation

This means watching what is happening, but watching with a purpose. You can't watch everything and you can end up just describing what happened. The observation needs to be very focused. You need to agree on who and what will be observed, and how often the observer will make a note of what they are looking for. A few headings will give structure to the exercise. Ideally, the observer should be someone who will be trusted and received positively by the artist and by those taking part. An observer can give useful feedback to an artist or workshop leader, as well as watching participants during the project.

For example, the Education Projects Officer of Birmingham Royal Ballet tracked three children taking part in a dance session with a Bhangra dance artist, as part of a joint project with SAMPAD. She noted her observations under three headings:

- focus and attention during the session
- technical development
- performance skills

These related to the objectives of the project, agreed between Birmingham Royal Ballet, SAMPAD and the Bhangra artist.

Online websites, chat rooms and email

You can use your website or email address to ask for feedback on particular activities. This can be done through open comments on email, or by asking users to complete a short questionnaire, returned online. You can set up Yahoo groups, which are open only to people who register through your adminstrator; these allow people taking part in a project to communicate securely with each other, exchange ideas and give their opinions on the activity.

You should be aware of the safeguarding issues when using the internet. Chatrooms, newsrooms or groups, email lists and interactive games can present particular risks, as child sex offenders can use them as a means to access children. You should carefully monitor the access and use of the internet when working with children or young people and in promoting the activities you are involved in. These issues are discussed in *Keeping Arts Safe*, Arts Council England, 2003 and see also the Home Office site www.thinkuknow.co.uk

Participatory techniques

Drama-based activities and games can help you collect evidence from those taking part in informal and enjoyable ways which don't disrupt the project and make people feel uncomfortably aware that they are now taking part in evaluation. Techniques can be as simple as asking people to show interest by raising their hands, or can involve more complicated role playing. Some of the techniques of theatre-in-education, such as putting someone, perhaps the artist, in the 'hot seat' to be questioned by the group, can reveal a great deal about how much participants have learned or developed through an activity.

> *For example,* Lawnmowers Theatre Company used drama and participatory techniques with adults with learning disabilities during their night club project. General strength of feeling on certain issues was measured by asking people who felt strongly about or were particularly interested in a subject or activity to stand closest to a certain spot; those who felt less strongly were asked to stand further away; those who did not feel strongly at all were asked to stand as far away as they could from the spot.

Participatory techniques are not always suited to providing permanent evidence, although you could consider using video or photography in partnership with them as long as this did not inhibit people's spontaneous reactions. They may be best used as an informal method of reviewing a project as it progresses.

Photography

Photography can be a very valuable tool in arts education projects, and the widespread use of digital cameras has made it a cheap and accessible medium, with instant results. Time-lapse photography – taking photos at agreed intervals, say every 20 minutes – can provide useful evidence of change and the enjoyment of a project. You can track individuals or a larger group. Photography can record what is made or performed at the end of a project. People taking part can make their own record of a project, which may be useful for both documentation and evaluation.

For example, during weekly sessions of the Puffins Nursery music and dance project, *The Very Hungry Caterpillar,* photographs were taken at 20-minute intervals and illustrated the whole process. Three photographs were selected from each week for evaluation. They showed how the children gradually acquired music and dance skills (an aim of the project). They also showed some unplanned 'magical moments' and exploratory work.

You should be aware of the safeguarding issues in using photographs of children, young people and vulnerable adults, especially online, where individuals should never be named identified by name, address or distinguishing marks. You should seek parental consent before using images in any public printed or online form. The Arts Council England publication, *Keeping Arts Safe* gives more information (see Appendix 6).

Questionnaires

Questionnaires can take a variety of forms. They can be simple sheets with a few questions needing yes/no or agree/disagree answers or asking for a score or rating. These can give straightforward quantitative evidence which is easy to interpret and use.

> *For example,* a question using scoring might be:
>
> How would you rate the photography sessions overall?
>
> Excellent 10 9 8 7 6 5 4 3 2 1 Poor   *Please circle a score*
>
> This will lead to information like:
> 75% of the young people rated the photography session highly at 8 or above
> (20 young people took part)
>
> A yes/no question could be:
>
> I have improved my skills in using a camera.   Yes ☐ No ☐ *Please tick box*
>
> Information gained from this evidence would be:
> 50% of the young people felt they had improved their camera skills

You can also include a list of possible answers, and ask people to tick which ones they agree with. Again, the answers will be straightforward to interpret, and likely to yield quantitative evidence.

> *For example,* the pupils' questionnaire for *Off the Wall*, an arts education project at Dewsbury Town Hall, managed by Kirklees Cultural Services, included this question:
>
> Did you learn anything new about any of the following?
>
> | | |
> |---|---|
> | Composing music | [ ] |
> | Making shadow puppets | [ ] |
> | Photography | [ ] |
> | Taking part in a performance | [ ] |
> | Dewsbury Town Hall | [ ] |
> | Working with people | [ ] |

Questionnaires also allow for answers to more 'open' questions beginning Who, What, Why, Where, When and How, which cannot be answered simply yes or no. These will give more qualitative evidence. This kind of evidence will be more in-depth and give you some lively quotes, but it is more difficult to pull together, and will certainly be more time-consuming to interpret. People may also be less likely to spend the time answering more searching questions, rather than ticking a range of options or circling a score. A combination of scoring or tick boxes and open questions can be effective.

For example, on a questionnaire for teachers following an animation project at Cavendish First School, Artworks used a combined approach of scoring and open questions. These referred to different aspects of the project, such as aims and objectives, the creative process, and project management.

Process

What went well and why? _____

_____

What didn't go well and why? _____

_____

Please circle how successful you feel this area of the project was

5	4	3	2	I
Fantastic	Good	OK	Not too good	Terrible

Analysis of the answers

All 3 teachers rated the process highly at 5

Comments included:

- *All children, whatever their ability were able to contribute to the creative process.*
- *They could all understand what they were supposed to be doing, and why.*
- *The soundtrack aspect was too hurried, but this was discussed and the project could not have been handled any better.*
- *I thought the little bits of process I was involved in were really exciting.*

You can use pictures and diagrams on questionnaires or feedback sheets for people with limited literacy skills. Examples might be circling or colouring faces with a range of different expressions.

You need to give out enough questionnaires to make sure you get sufficient responses for your evidence to be convincing. If questionnaires are filled in away from the project, the average rate of return is 20% – 25%. You should always make it clear how many people took part, and how many of these returned the questionnaire, so that it is clear on what you are basing your conclusions.

When designing a questionnaire:

- test out a draft
- make sure questions are clear and can be understood by the people responding
- check that the questionnaire will tell you what you need to know
- check that you are not leading people to the answer you want
- always try to keep a questionnaire as short as possible – people will be more likely to complete it!
- check that someone has time to collate all the answers and make sense of them

Small group discussions

Small groups (about 7) can stimulate discussion and may help people to explore their experience of the project in more depth as they respond to others. As with interviews, have a set of questions ready to lead the debate and to make sure you find out what you want to know. Small group discussions can also be self-led. You can provide a set of questions, and ask the group to feed back to you what was said, rather than lead the discussion yourself.

For example, during the Dewsbury Town Hall project, Kirklees Cultural Services provided a prompt sheet for teachers to carry out interviews with small groups of pupils after the second session in school. The interviews were taped, and transcribed by a Kirklees Cultural Services officer, as teachers did not have time to do this.

When running small group discussions:

- choose a range of people for a balance of views and attitudes

- remember that some people may be more open if their group leader is not there. However, there are safeguarding issues with children, young people and vulnerable adults who cannot be left unsupervised by their carers. You may need to seek parental permission to interview children, young people and vulnerable adults. See the guide *Keeping Arts Safe* published by Arts Council England for more advice and information

- choose a quiet room, explain the agenda to the group, agree with them how their comments will be used and think about how to record what is said. As with individual interviews, taping the discussion provides a complete and accurate record, but is time-consuming to transcribe. If possible, organise a facilitator and a note-taker, so that the facilitator does not have to write during the meeting

- leave time to summarise and agree the main points at the end

Tape recordings

Tape recorders are useful at interviews and small group discussions (see above). They can also be used like a diary or comments' box/book to record the thoughts of artists or participants. Tape recorders are small and easy to use, and less intrusive than a video camera.

Video

You can use video to record the whole project for documentation purposes. Video can also be used to record interviews, small group discussions or private 'diary' sessions by artists or people taking part. These do not rely on writing skills. Using a structure, such as a set of questions, may help provide evidence which can be more easily compared and interpreted.

For example, during their project with Bath and Keynsham Young Carers, which aimed to produce a piece of theatre, ACTA Community Theatre used an unobtrusive 8mm video camera to record each session. All comments and presentations were recorded, as well as short feedback interviews at the end of each session to evaluate the most and least successful elements. Each session's highlights were roughly edited onto VHS before the planning meeting for the following week. One member of the group was uncomfortable with performing, and took on the filming responsibilities. All the filmed improvisation and devising was used as the basis for the final script. What started as an evaluative tool, ended up as an important part of the creative process of the project. This was an unexpected, but highly successful outcome, which will inform future projects.

You should be aware of the safe guarding issues in using video of children, young people and vulnerable adults, especially online, where individuals should never be identified by name, address or distinguishing marks. You should seek parental consent before using images in any public or online form. The Arts Council England publication, *Keeping Arts Safe* gives more information.

Written diary

The artist or group leader can make short daily notes on the progress of the project, perhaps organised under headings of high points and low points. People taking part can also keep a record in this way, noting their feelings and opinions about the project. However, you need to consider whether evidence gathered from 30 diaries is manageable once you come to assemble and interpret it all. Also, people may be reluctant to share what they have written, and prefer to keep diaries private.

For example, children taking part in weekly drama workshops at the Mercury Theatre, Colchester, used personal diaries to record their reactions to each session. Entries show what activities the children enjoyed, what they found boring and how their confidence grew.

Week 1.   *I really liked today. I was a bit nervous at first, but the instructors made me feel welcome.*

Week 2.   *I came today with a lot more confidence than last week. We played the mirror game together. I like the mirror game.*

Week 7.   *We have now started another new topic, where we are making a poster about dropping litter. I find this very boring*

Appendix 4
Pilot groups

The following groups and organisations piloted the first edition of the Guide, and their projects have provided many of the examples in the text.

ACTA Community Theatre, Bristol

Action Factory Community Arts, Blackburn

Artists in Schools, Inspection, Support and Advisory Service, Bradford MBC

Arts Access, Gloucester

Bolton, Bury and Rochdale Artists in Schools

Chichester Festival Theatre

Fabrica, Brighton

Hartlepool Borough Council Community Services

Isle of Wight Council, Youth Arts Partnership

John Masefield High School, Ledbury

Kirklees Cultural Services

Lawnmowers, Newcastle-upon-Tyne

Mercury Theatre, Colchester

Music and Dance Education Trust, Truro

Nottingham City Museums and Galleries Access Team

Reckless Sleepers, Nottingham

SAMPAD, Birmingham

Signals Media Arts, Colchester

Appendix 5

Contacting Arts Council England

phone: 0845 300 6200

www.artscouncil.org.uk

Regional Offices	Area covered
Arts Council England *National Office* 14 Great Peter Street London SW1P 3NQ Phone: 020 7333 0100 Fax: 020 7973 6590 Textphone: 020 7973 6564	Bedfordshire, Cambridgeshire, Essex, Hertfordshire, Norfolk, Suffolk; unitary authorities of Luton, Peterborough, Southend-on-Sea, Thurrock.
Arts Council England *East* 48-49 Bateman Street Cambridge CB2 1LR Phone: 01223 454400 Fax: 0870 242 1271 Textphone: 01223 306893	Bedfordshire, Cambridgeshire, Essex, Hertfordshire, Norfolk, Suffolk; and unitary authorities of Luton, Peterborough, Southend-on-Sea, Thurrock
Arts Council England *East Midlands* St Nicholas Court 25-27 Castle Gate Nottingham NG1 7AR Phone: 0115 989 7520 Fax: 0115 950 2467	Derbyshire, Leicestershire, Lincolnshire (excluding North and North East Lincolnshire), Northamptonshire, Nottinghamshire; and unitary authorities of Derby, Leicester, Nottingham, Rutland
Arts Council England *London* 2 Pear Tree Court London EC1R 0DS Phone: 020 7608 6100 Fax: 020 7608 4100 Textphone: 020 7608 4101	Greater London
Arts Council England *North East* Central Square Forth Street Newcastle upon Tyne NE1 3PJ Phone: 0191 255 8500 Fax: 0191 230 1020 Textphone: 0191 255 8500	Durham, Northumberland; metropolitan authorities of Gateshead, Newcastle upon Tyne, North Tyneside, South Tyneside, Sunderland; and unitary authorities of Darlington, Hartlepool, Middlesbrough, Redcar and Cleveland, Stockton-on-Tees.

Regional Offices	Area covered
Arts Council England *North West* Manchester House 22 Bridge Street Manchester M3 3AB Phone: 0161 834 6644 Fax: 0161 834 6969 Textphone: 0161 834 9131	Cheshire, Cumbria, Lancashire; metropolitan authorities of Bolton, Bury, Knowsley, Liverpool, Manchester, Oldham, Rochdale, St Helens, Salford, Sefton, Stockport, Tameside, Trafford, Wigan, Wirral; and unitary authorities of Blackburn with Darwen, Blackpool, Halton, Warrington
Arts Council England *South East* Sovereign House Church Street Brighton BN1 1RA Phone: 01273 763000 Fax: 0870 242 1257 Textphone: 01273 710659	Buckinghamshire, East Sussex, Hampshire, Isle of Wight, Kent, Oxfordshire, Surrey, West Sussex; and unitary authorities of Bracknell Forest, Brighton & Hove, Medway, Milton Keynes, Portsmouth, Reading, Slough, Southampton, West Berkshire, Windsor and Maidenhead, Wokingham
Arts Council England *South West* Bradninch Place Gandy Street Exeter EX4 3LS Tel: 01392 218 188 Fax: 01392 229229 Textphone: 01392 433503	Cornwall, Devon, Dorset, Gloucestershire and Somerset; unitary authorities of Bath and North East Somerset, Wiltshire, Isle of Scilly, Poole, Swindon, Bristol, North Somerset, Plymouth, South Gloucestershire, Torbay.
Arts Council England *West Midlands* 82 Granville Street Birmingham B1 2LH Tel: 0121 631 3121 Fax: 0121 643 7239 Textphone: 0121 643 2815	Shropshire, Staffordshire, Warwickshire, Worcestershire; metropolitan authorities of Birmingham, Coventry, Dudley, Sandwell, Solihull, Walsall, Wolverhampton; and unitary authorities of Herefordshire, Stoke-on-Trent, Telford and Wrekin
Arts Council England *Yorkshire* 21 Bond Street Dewsbury West Yorkshire WF13 1AX Phone: 01924 455555 Fax: 01924 466522 or 0870 242 1267 Textphone: 01924 438585	North Yorkshire; metropolitan authorities of Barnsley, Bradford, Calderdale, Doncaster, Kirklees, Leeds, Rotherham, Sheffield, Wakefield; and unitary authorities of East Riding of Yorkshire, Kingston upon Hull, North Lincolnshire, North East Lincolnshire, York

Appendix 6
Additional resources

Built-in, not bolt-on: engaging young people in evaluation and consultation, Madeline Swords, New Opportunities Fund, 2002. Discussion of effective ways of consulting with young people, with practical suggestions of how to engage young people in evaluation. Can be downloaded from *www.nof.org.uk* Follow links to research and evaluation, and then publications; look for Engaging Young People Full Report.

Guidelines for research among children and young people, Market Research Society, 2000. A helpful code of conduct for carrying out research when working with children and young people. It can be downloaded from *www.mrs.org.uk/standards/children.htm*

Keeping Arts Safe; protection of children, young people and vulnerable adults involved in arts activities, Arts Council England, 2003. A practical guide to safeguarding issues, including when and how to use the Criminal Records Bureau for police checks, frequently asked questions and useful proformas. It can be downloaded from *www.artscouncil.org.uk/information/publications.php* Additional resources on safeguarding can be found on the website of the National Society for the Prevention of Cruelty to Children at *www.nspcc.org.uk*

Practical monitoring and evaluation: a guide for voluntary organisations, Charities Evaluation Service, 2004. A comprehensive guide to monitoring and evaluation aimed at small and medium sized voluntary organisations. You can buy the full guide (Basic, Advanced and Toolkit) or the shorter basic set (Basic and Toolkit) from Charities Evaluation Services, 4 Coldbath Square, London EC1R 5HL. See also *www.ces-vol.org.uk/html/bookshop.htm* The website lists many other useful publications on evaluation and quality assurance, and explains the training opportunities offered by the Charities Evaluation Services.

Scottish Arts Council e-tool for evaluation *www.evaluationforall.org.uk* Scottish Arts Council has produced an interactive guide to evaluation designed to help improve and develop practice. You can use the toolkit to plan and develop your evaluation or explore specific information and examples. It is based on the five stage approach of *Partnerships for Learning*.

Sharing practice: a guide to self-evaluation for artists, arts organisations and funders working in the context of social exclusion, Gerri Moriarty, Arts Council England, 2002. Focuses on the processes used by arts organisations, individual practitioners and participants to reflect on and develop their practice. Can be downloaded from *www.newaudiences.org.uk/downloads/btp_sharing_practice.doc*

UK Evaluation Society's website lists many online evaluation resources. *www.evaluation.org.uk/Pub_library/Online_eval.htm*

Working in partnership: a sourcebook, New Opportunities Fund, 2002 Detailed and practical guidance on working in partnership across many different sectors, including a section on self-evaluation. Useful checklists and further resources. Can be downloaded from *www.nof.org.uk* Follow links to research and evaluation, and then publications. On the same site see also, *Self-evaluation: a handy guide to sources*, 2003.

Glossary

Aims	the main purposes of a project, i.e. why the project is taking place
Analysis	interpreting data and evidence to provide information on which to base judgements
Data	evidence which has not been interpreted
Documentation	a complete descriptive record of what happened
Evaluation	making judgements, based on evidence, about the value and quality of a project
Evidence	data gathered during a project which can be used as a basis for evaluation
Information	statements based on the interpretation of data
Learning outcomes	what is learned as a result of the arts project, such as gains in knowledge and understanding of, or skills in, the arts, or personal and social change
Measures of success	how you will know if an objective has been achieved, and ways of measuring the learning outcomes of a project. They are also sometimes called performance indicators, success criteria or outcomes

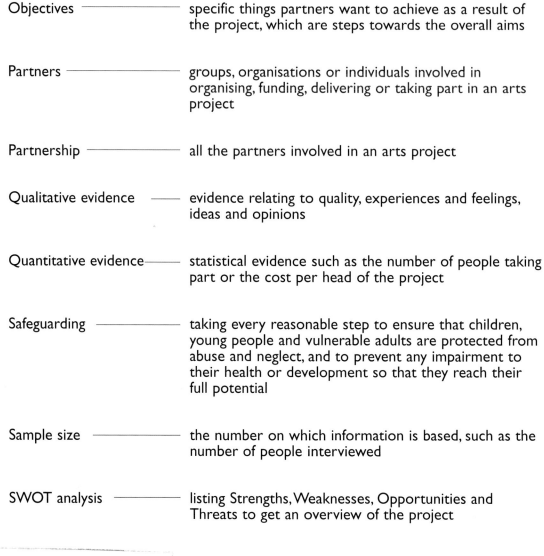

Objectives ——————— specific things partners want to achieve as a result of the project, which are steps towards the overall aims

Partners ——————— groups, organisations or individuals involved in organising, funding, delivering or taking part in an arts project

Partnership ——————— all the partners involved in an arts project

Qualitative evidence —— evidence relating to quality, experiences and feelings, ideas and opinions

Quantitative evidence——— statistical evidence such as the number of people taking part or the cost per head of the project

Safeguarding ——————— taking every reasonable step to ensure that children, young people and vulnerable adults are protected from abuse and neglect, and to prevent any impairment to their health or development so that they reach their full potential

Sample size ——————— the number on which information is based, such as the number of people interviewed

SWOT analysis ——————— listing Strengths, Weaknesses, Opportunities and Threats to get an overview of the project